D1465680

★

FUN & CREATIVE
WORKSHOP ACTIVITIES

COOL
LEATHERWORKING
PROJECTS

REBECCA FELIX

Checkerboard Library

An Imprint of Abdo Publishing
abdopublishing.com

ABDOPUBLISHING.COM

Published by Abdo Publishing, a division of ABDO, PO Box 398166, Minneapolis, Minnesota 55439. Copyright © 2017 by Abdo Consulting Group, Inc. International copyrights reserved in all countries. No part of this book may be reproduced in any form without written permission from the publisher. Checkerboard Library™ is a trademark and logo of Abdo Publishing.

Printed in the United States of America, North Mankato, Minnesota
062016
092016

Design and Production: Mighty Media, Inc.
Series Editor: Paige V. Polinsky
Photo Credits: Rebecca Felix, Paige V. Polinsky, Shutterstock

The following manufacturers/names appearing in this book are trademarks: Crafter's Pick™, Elmer's® CraftBond®, Sharpie®

Library of Congress Cataloging-in-Publication Data

Names: Felix, Rebecca, 1984- author.
Title: Cool leatherworking projects : fun & creative workshop activities / Rebecca Felix.
Description: Minneapolis, Minnesota : Abdo Publishing, [2017] | Series: Cool industrial arts | Includes bibliographical references and index.
Identifiers: LCCN 2016006197 (print) | LCCN 2016007327 (ebook) | ISBN 9781680781281 (print) | ISBN 9781680775488 (ebook)
Subjects: LCSH: Leatherwork--Juvenile literature.
Classification: LCC TT290 .F45 2017 (print) | LCC TT290 (ebook) | DDC 745.53/1--dc23
LC record available at http://lccn.loc.gov/2016006197

TO ADULT HELPERS

This is your chance to help children learn about industrial arts! They will also develop new skills, gain confidence, and make cool things. These activities are designed to teach children how to work with leather. Readers may need more assistance for some activities than others. Be there to offer guidance when they need it. Encourage them to do as much as they can on their own. Be a cheerleader for their creativity!

Look at the beginning of each project for its difficulty rating (EASY, INTERMEDIATE, ADVANCED).

TABLE OF CONTENTS

WHAT

IS LEATHERWORKING?

Leatherworking is making things out of leather. Shoes, belts, coats, and more can be made of leather. Leather is treated animal skin. Some leather is very soft and lightweight. It might become a thin bracelet or cover a pillow. Other leather is tough and thick. It can be used to create horse saddles or sturdy work boots.

LEATHERWORKING TECHNIQUES

Workshop Tips

It is important to set up a safe, clean workspace when working with leather. The most important part of a workshop is a flat, hard surface. It could be in the garage, in the basement, or at the kitchen table. Just make sure you get **permission**! Then, follow the tips below to work safely.

- Tools should be within easy reach and stored in safe places.

- Wear gloves when using sharp tools to cut leather.

- Make sure there is enough light to see well.

- Work in an area that is well **ventilated**.

- Keep your workspace clean and free of clutter.

Essential Safety Gear

- Gloves

- Safety goggles

- Face mask

- Closed-toe shoes

Be Prepared

- Read the entire project before you begin.

- Make sure you have everything you need to do the project.

- Follow the directions carefully.

- Clean up after you are finished.

ADULT HELPERS

Working with leather can be **dangerous**. It can require the use of sharp tools and strong glues and chemicals. That means you should have an adult standing by for some of these projects.

KEY SYMBOLS

In this book, you will see some symbols above the project material lists. Here is what they mean:

HOT!
This project requires hot tools. Handle with caution.

FACE MASK
Doing this project creates dust or requires glues with strong odors. A face mask should be worn for protection.

TOOLS OF THE TRADE

Here are some of the materials you will need for the projects in this book.

**ADHESIVE
HOOK & LOOP TAPE**

BINDER CLIPS

COFFEE CAN

DUCT TAPE

FABRIC GLUE

FISHING LINE

**HOT GLUE GUN &
GLUE STICKS**

LACING NEEDLE

LEATHER

LEATHER LACE

LEATHER ROTARY
PUNCH

PAPER

PENCIL

RAG

ROCK

RUBBER CEMENT

RUBBING ALCOHOL

RULER

STICK PENS

THREE-RING FOLDER

LEATHER LACE PEN WRAPS

WRAP PENS IN
LEATHER FOR AWESOME
GRIP AND COOL
SCHOOL-TOOL STYLE!

MATERIALS

- 50" (152.4 cm) leather lace, 1 to 3 colors
- ruler
- scissors
- pen

1. To wrap a pen in one color, cut a piece of leather 50 inches (152.4 cm) long. For two colors, cut one 30-inch (76 cm) piece of each color. For three colors, cut one 20-inch (50.8 cm) piece of each color.

2. Start wrapping a piece of leather around the pen. After a few wraps, loosen the first loop. Tuck the short tail under it. Pull it tight.

3. Continue wrapping the leather tightly around the pen.

4. To change colors, loosen the last loop. Tuck the tail under the loop and pull tight. Repeat step 2 with another color.

5. Wrap the entire pen. Then loosen the last loop and tuck in the tail.

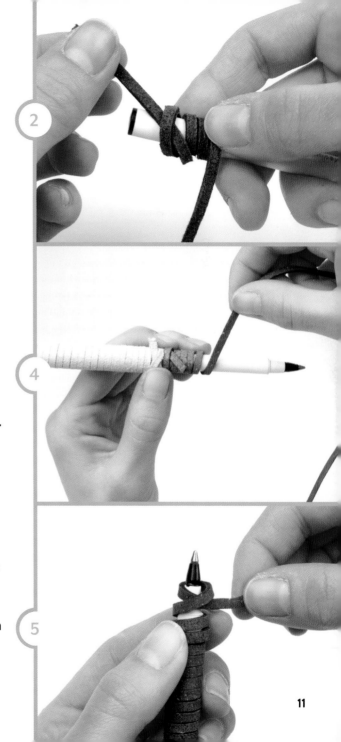

11

BRAIDED GARLAND

LONG ROPES OF
BRAIDED LEATHER
WILL HOLD TASSELS,
FEATHERS, FRAMES,
AND ANY OTHER
TRINKETS YOU LIKE!

MATERIALS

- scissors
- leather lace,
  1 to 3 colors
- ruler
- duct tape
- leather scraps
- pushpin
- fishing line
- photos,
  pom-poms,
  and other
  trinkets

DIFFICULTY
EASY

BRAIDING

1 Cut three pieces of leather lace a bit longer than you want your **garland** to be. Some length will be lost as you braid the pieces.

2 Tie the three pieces of lace in a knot at one end. Use duct tape to secure the knot to a table.

3 Braid the laces. Tie the ends in a knot.

Continued on the next page.

13

DECORATING

1 Cut fringe, feathers, or shapes out of leather scraps. The shapes can be used as frames. Roll small pieces of duct tape with the sticky side out. Use them to attach pictures to the leather shapes.

2 Use the pushpin to make a hole near the top of each shape. Cut short pieces of fishing line and thread them through the pushpin holes. Tie the shapes to the **garland**.

3 Use the fishing line to tie **trinkets** to the garland. You can add as many trinkets and leather shapes as you wish!

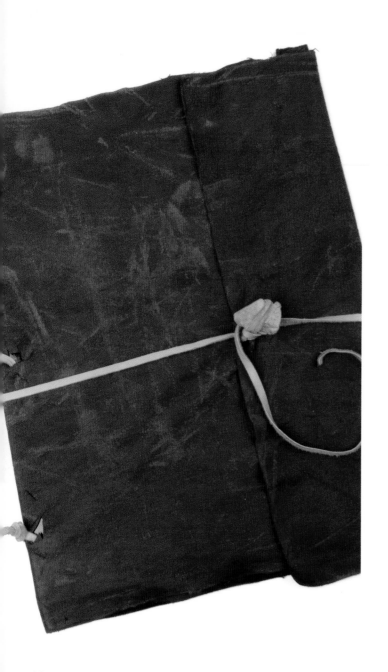

MEDIEVAL FOLDER

DISTRESS A PIECE OF LEATHER TO CREATE AN ANCIENT FOLDER COVER!

MATERIALS

- ruler
- marker
- leather
- scissors
- face mask
- rubber gloves
- rubbing alcohol
- old rag
- sandpaper (any coarseness)
- three-ring folder
- 4 to 5 binder clips
- leather rotary punch
- 60" (152.4 cm) of leather lace
- hot glue gun & glue sticks
- small rock

CUTTING + DISTRESSING

1 Lay the open folder on the leather. Mark 1 inch (2.5 cm) above and 4 inches (10 cm) out on one side of the folder. Draw and cut out a leather rectangle using these marks.

2 Put on the face mask and gloves. Use the rag to work rubbing alcohol into the leather until it's damp. Let the leather dry completely.

3 Twist the leather to make wrinkles. Hold the wrinkles in place and rub them with sandpaper. Twist the leather into new shapes and sand some more.

Continued on the next page.

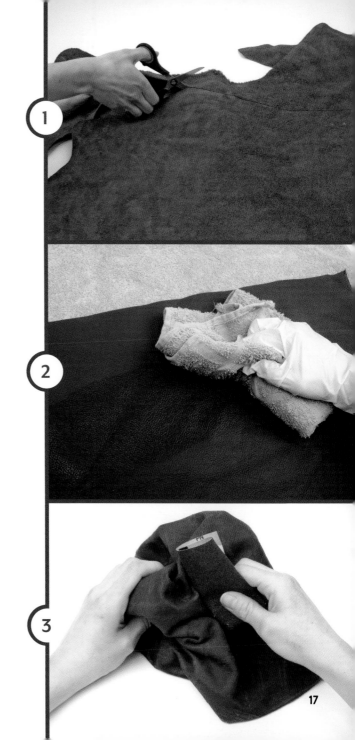

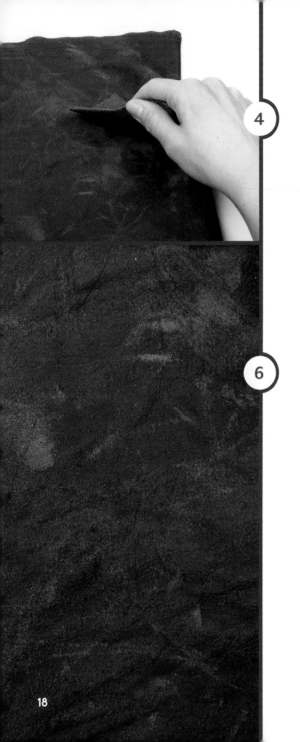

4 Lay the leather flat. Keep **distressing** the leather with sandpaper.

5 Take the leather outside. Stomp on it in the dirt! Drag it across the sidewalk. Rub it on trees.

6 Repeat steps 2 through 5 until the leather looks as worn as you want.

TIP

Some leather may be more difficult to distress, due to its finish or thickness. Keep trying! Twist and crumple your leather, soak it in water, or scratch it with a brush! Eventually, it will look aged.

ATTACHING TO
THE FOLDER

1 Lay the open folder on top of the leather. Place it so the left edge of the folder is ½ inch (1.3 cm) in from the edge of the leather. Use a binder clip to hold the folder in place.

2 Fold the wider edge of the leather over the folder. Use a binder clip to hold the flap in place.

3 Close the folder. Use your fingers to feel for the folder's holes under the leather. Mark the three spots on the front of the folder.

Continued on the next page.

4 Keep the folder closed and use the leather rotary punch to make holes through the marks.

5 Cut three 7-inch (17.8 cm) pieces of leather lace. Thread one piece through each punched hole. Knot together and trim the ends.

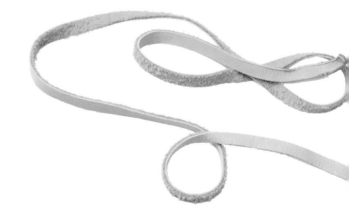

6 Open the folder. Fold the leather flap hanging off the left side over onto the folder. Use hot glue to secure the flap onto the folder. Use binder clips to hold the flap in place as it dries.

7 Remove the binder clips from the right side of the folder. Place a line of hot glue on the leather along the back edge of the folder.

8 Press the folder onto the leather. The wider flap should remain loose and sticking out from the right edge of the folder. Let the glue dry.

Continued on the next page.

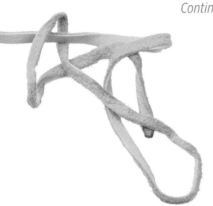

CREATING THE TIE

1 Measure about halfway down the right flap. Use the leather rotary punch to make a hole.

2 Tie the rock onto the remaining leather lace about 5 inches (12.7 cm) from one end. Then thread the short end of the lace through the hole and tie a knot.

3 Close the folder. Wrap the long end of the lace around the folder to the right. Wind the lace around the rock to hold the folder closed. Have fun using your **medieval**-looking creation!

TIP
Do you have a wood-burning tool? Use it to burn designs or drawings into the leather!

BACKPACK POUCH

MAKE A MINI LEATHER POUCH TO LATCH ONTO YOUR BACKPACK STRAP!

MATERIALS

- marker
- construction paper
- ruler
- scissors
- leather
- binder clips
- rotary leather punch

- 2 10" (25 cm) pieces of skinny leather lace
- at least 15" (38.1 cm) of hook & loop tape
- leather scraps
- fabric glue

MAKING THE TEMPLATE

1 Draw a 3-by-11-inch (7.5-by-28 cm) rectangle in the middle of the paper. Mark the bottom with a B.

2 Draw a line across the paper 2 inches (5 cm) from the top of the rectangle. Draw another line 3 inches (7.5 cm) below that. Cut out the *t* shape.

3 Draw a horizontal line 1 inch (2.5 cm) below the top of the crosspiece. Draw another line 1 inch (2.5 cm) below that. Cut out the middle rectangles on each side of the crosspiece.

4 The paper cutout is the **template**. Trace it onto the leather. Cut the leather shape out.

CUTTING, STITCHING + FINISHING

1 Lay the leather shape flat. Fold the bottom up so it is even with the top flaps. Secure it with binder clips.

2 Draw eight or ten dots along each side of the pouch. Use the rotary punch to make a hole through each dot. Be sure to go through both layers of leather. Remove the binder clips.

3 Tie a knot in one end of each piece of leather lace. Use the lace to stitch the leather, one on each side. After the final hole on each side, tie the end in a knot.

4 Stick scratchy hook-and-loop tape to the front of the left flaps. Stick fuzzy hook-and-loop tape to the back of the right flaps.

5 Stick hook-and-loop tape to the top flap and front of the pouch. This will keep the pouch closed. Cut leather scraps into fun shapes. Glue them onto the pouch. Let the glue dry.

6 Fill your pouch and attach it to a backpack strap!

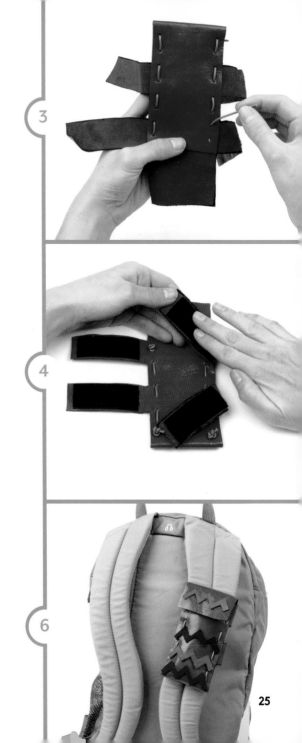

LEATHER
HOBBY CADDY

MAKE A
LEATHER-WRAPPED
CADDY WITH
DETACHABLE
POCKETS THAT HOLD
HOBBY SUPPLIES!

MATERIALS

- coffee can
- ruler
- marker
- leather
- scissors
- face mask
- rubber cement
- 9 binder clips
- hook & loop tape
- stapler
- rotary leather punch
- leather lace
- lacing needle

WRAPPING THE CAN

1. Measure the height of the can. Add 2 inches (5 cm). Write the total measurement down.

2. Measure the **diameter** of the can's opening. Multiply the diameter by four. Write the total measurement down.

3. Draw a rectangle on the leather using the measurements from steps 1 and 2. Cut out the rectangle.

4. Put on the face mask. Paint the can with rubber cement.

5. Wrap the leather around the can. Work slowly to make sure the bottom of the can lines up with the edge of the leather. Let the rubber cement dry.

Continued on the next page.

27

6 Make eight cuts in the leather above the can. Space the cuts evenly. End the cuts before the edge of the can.

7 Paint rubber cement on the inside of each leather flap. Fold the flaps down inside the can. Use binder clips to clamp the flaps to the lip of the can. Let the glue dry.

8 Remove the clips. If you have any leftover leather scraps, cut them into different shapes. Glue them around the can in a fun pattern! Let the glue dry.

9 Cut a piece of scratchy hook-and-loop tape to circle the inside of the can. Stick it inside the can, just below the rim.

MAKING POCKETS

1 Cut several rectangles out of leather. Fold one end of a rectangle up to make a pocket. Staple the sides.

2 Fold one end of another rectangle. Use the rotary punch to make holes through both layers of the leather, along each side.

3 Use leather lace to stitch one side of the pocket. Tie a knot after the final hole. Repeat on the other side.

Continued on the next page.

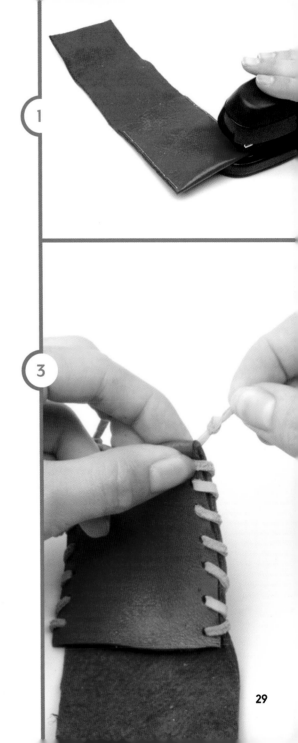

4 Make more pockets using either of the methods from steps 1 through 3.

5 Attach fuzzy pieces of hook-and-loop tape to the top back edge of each pocket.

6 Hang the pockets on the can using the hook-and-loop tape. Fill the **caddy** and pockets with art supplies!

GLOSSARY

CADDY – a container for storing or holding objects when they are not in use.

DANGEROUS – able or likely to cause harm or injury.

DIAMETER – the distance across the middle of a circle.

DISTRESS – to scratch, damage, or rough up fabric or wood to make it look aged.

GARLAND – a decorative ring or rope made of leaves, flowers, or some other material.

MEDIEVAL – of or belonging to the Middle Ages. The Middle Ages was a period in European history from about 500 CE to 1500 CE.

PERMISSION – when a person in charge says it is okay to do something.

TEMPLATE – a shape or pattern that is drawn or cut around to make the same shape in another material.

TRINKET – a small item of little value.

VENTILATE – to allow fresh air to enter and move through a room.

Websites

To learn more about Cool Industrial Arts, visit **booklinks.abdopublishing.com**. These links are routinely monitored and updated to provide the most current information available.

INDEX

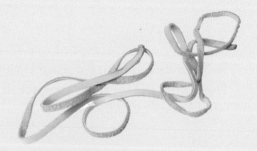